Home Beermaking
The Complete Beginner's Guidebook

Home Beermaking
The Complete Beginner's Guidebook

By William Moore

Third Edition

Ferment Press
San Leandro
California

Published by:
Ferment Press
P.O. Box 2195
San Leandro, CA 94577

First printing, third edition: January 1991
Second printing, third edition: February 1992

ISBN: 0-9605318-1-5

Illustrations by Jeanne Carlson
Cover photographs by Tom Poole
Layout by Jay Hershel

Thanks to Monica

Printed in the United States of America

Contents

1 Beers of the World

Lager Beer

Brewed with bottom-fermenting yeast and aged under refrigeration, lager is the most popular beer in the world. Lager is more difficult than ale or steam beer to brew at home, as refrigerated aging and high quality lager yeast are required. The term lager is of German origin and means "to store". Breweries in Europe generally store their lager for 4 to 12 weeks in refrigerated cellars before marketing, allowing the beer to develop a very smooth taste, free of the oxidizing influence of warmer temperatures. Stronger European-style lagers can take 2 months or more to mature under refrigeration, while some of the lighter (and cheaper) lagers are only aged 2 to 3 weeks under refrigeration. Although there are as many lagers as there are towns in Germany, the principal styles are listed below.

Dry Beer originated in Japan, and is a light lager that has been force-fermented with genetically altered yeast to a very low final gravity. The special yeast eats much of the body and sweetness producing dextrins that normally remain in beer, resulting in a beer with very little sweetness, perceived by the mouth as a lack of lingering aftertaste. Dry beer has not yet become popular with home brewers, probably due to both a lack of interest and lack of the special yeast strain needed.

1

Light Lager (color, not calories) is brewed from pale malted barley and usually has a mellow, crisp character. Examples include Budweiser, Heineken, and Germanys Beck's Light.

Pilsener is a variety of light lager traditionally made from soft water and flavored solely with Saaz hops. An extremely flavorful beer with a pronounced hop character, the most famous example is Pilsner Urquell, brewed in Pilsnen, Czechoslovakia. The Pilsner Urquell brewery is unique in that it malts its own barley, and uses 4 different strains of yeast to ferment its outstanding pilsner.

Dark Lager is made from pale malted barley and roasted malted barley. It is usually sweeter than light lager and has a smooth caramelized or slightly roasted malt flavor. Examples include Heineken Dark and Lowenbrau Dark.

Bock is the traditional spring beer of Germany. Well-made bock is heavy and usually dark with a sweet malt flavor. Bock, originally brewed in the German town of Einbeck, is often labeled commercially with a goat symbol, (especially by breweries outside of Germany) as bock is the word for male goat in several Germanic languages. The name bock when referring to beer, however, is probably the result of centuries of beer-soaked mispronunciation of the last syllable of Einbeck, rather than a German brewer's tribute to the billy-goat.

Steam-style Beer

Steam beer, the only native American beer style, was born in late 19th century San Francisco, when refrigeration and ice were unavailable to Eastern immigrants accustomed to lager brewing. Desiring local beer, they brewed with lager yeast at ale (unrefrigerated) temperatures, producing a robust, highly hopped (partly for preservative reasons) brew more like an ale than a lager in flavor, yet with a unique sharp character imparted by the warm-fermenting lager yeast. Unlike most draft beers at the time, steam beer was carbonated (by krausening), and the hissing noise issuing from a freshly-tapped keg probably gave rise to the name steam.

Today, steam is a trademark of Anchor Brewing Company in San Francisco. Anchor's beer is an excellent robust amber beer, brewed with pure barley malt and flavored with a generous dose of whole Northern Brewer hops. Although Anchor makes an outstanding example, the word steam when referring to beer is now their trademark. Now that

3

steam is a trademark, its commercial development has been stifled, although home brewers can make and enjoy this unique half lager, half ale brew, and still call it by its proper name, steam beer.

Wheat Beer

Wheat beer is beer brewed with malted wheat in addition to malted barley, giving the beer a unique, soft, bread-like malt character. Unlike malted barley, malted wheat is huskless and consequently cannot impart the 'grainy' astringent flavor which can be leached from the husks of barley malt during the rinsing (sparging) process. Though strongly identified with Germany, it is believed wheat beer originated accidently in England, by brewers who could not separate the volunteer wheat from the barley commingling in their fields and consequently in their mash tuns.

Though there are several styles of wheat beer in Germany and Belgium, the most popular is the Weizenbier of southern Germany, a lager-like beer with a mild hop character and smooth flavor. Considered a refreshing summer beverage, wheat beer is enjoying a rise in popularity in both Germany and the United States, and both the August Schell Brewing Company of Minnesota and Grant's Brewing Company of Washington produce excellent examples.

Ale

Brewed with top-fermenting yeast, ale is of British origin, and often has a more pronounced flavor than lager. Ale is an extremely forgiving and easy style of beer to brew at home, as it does not require refrigerated aging, and good quality dried ale yeast is readily available. Like lager, there are many different styles of ale.

Pale ale represents the very best in English beer - a strong, generously hopped beer with a dry crisp taste. The finest hops are generally reserved by British brewers for inclusion in their pale ales. The most famous in our country (though milder and sweeter than the British version) is the imported Bass Pale Ale, brewed by the Bass Breweries, Burton-On-Trent, England. Many of the growing number of excellent regional brewers in the United States and Canada produce pale ales, and Sierra Nevada's Pale Ale (brewed in Chico, California) is one of the best examples. India pale ale (IPA) is a highly hopped version of pale ale, originally brewed by the British to survive the long and hot voyage to their then-colony of India.

Bitter, though rare in the United States, is the most popular draft beer in England. A milder, draft version of pale ale, bitter, despite its suggestive name, generally has less hop flavor, and consequently a sweeter flavor, than pale ale. Bitter is at its best when fresh and on draft (with just a hint of carbonation), as the higher carbonation levels expected of bottled beers tend to disrupt its smooth, malty flavor. Extra special bitter (ESB) is a stronger and more expensive version of bitter, generally with a more pronounced hop character.

Brown Ale is a sweet and dark amber bottled beer. It has a sweet caramelized flavor with only a hint of hop taste. Browns traditionally have a lower carbonation and alcohol level than most bottled beers. Newcastle Brown Ale from England is the most popular example in the United States.

Like brown ale, Mild Ale is a traditional working class English beer. Though displaced by bitter in Southern England in the last 37 years, it is still very popular in the Manchester-Mersey area, where it is brewed in light and dark forms. Lower in alcohol than other ales, mild is usually dark, malty, and vaguely caramel-sweet in flavor.

Porter is a dark ale with a mild flavor, like a cross between a brown ale and a stout. Porter was probably first brewed in London, England, in 1722, perhaps in response to the then-popular pub practice of mixing the beers of two or three draft casks into one glass. A local brewer then developed a beer said to be like the blended pints served in pubs, and porter was born. The name porter was adopted gradually, perhaps due to the new beer's popularity among train porters. Porter brewing is enjoying a revival in the United States and Canada by a number of regional brewers, including the Sierra Nevada Brewing Company of Chico, California, and the Yuengling Brewing Company of Pottsville, Pennsylvania.

Stout is an extremely rich and creamy dark brew (almost black) made with the addition of roasted barley and or black patent malt. Irish stout (Guinness) is typically dry, while English stout can be quite sweet (Mackeson). Like porter, stout is enjoying a revival by the new regional brewers.

Strong Ale and Barley Wine are two names for very strong ales with starting gravities of at least 1.070. Traditionally made only in England, barley wine style beers are increasingly brewed by the newer regional brewers. Barley wine and strong ale are usually a deep amber color, balanced with a strong hop character.

2 Brewing Equipment

Sterilization

The importance of sterilization in brewing cannot be over-emphasized; everything coming in contact with the beer after boiling (fermenter, stirring spoon, hydrometer, thermometer, etc.) must be sterilized, because raw beer (called wort, and pronounced 'wert') is a very conducive medium for bacterial growth.

Chlorine is the most popular sterilant for brewing equipment. Chlorine-based cleaners (often supplemented with scrubbing agents) are usually available at home brewing stores or you can use unscented household laundry bleach, which contains chlorine. To make a working solution, add 2 tablespoons of unscented bleach to 1 gallon of water and cap to prevent chlorine evaporation. To use, rinse the equipment to be sterilized in the diluted solution, and then rinse with water to remove bleach traces before use.

Diluted unscented bleach is also excellent for periodically removing brown beer film from plastic fermenters - add 1 cup of unscented bleach to a 5 gallon fermenter, fill with water, and let sit overnight.

Scales

A small kitchen scale sensitive in the ounce range is needed when weighing hops, while a larger scale with a capacity of several pounds is helpful for weighing out malt extract, grain, and sugar.

The Brewing Kettle

A cooking pot of at least 3 gallons capacity (ideally 5 gallons) is needed to boil the malt and hops. Kettles larger than 3 gallons are preferable because they increase the amount of water that can be boiled with the malt, allowing for a more vigorous, cleansing boil, while reducing the risk of a messy boil over. The boiling pot should be made of stainless steel or enameled steel, as aluminum can react with the acid wort, possibly creating off-flavors. An aluminum pot is usable in a pinch, but should not be purchased for use in brewing. If you are purchasing a pot for use in brewing, select one of at least 5 gallons capacity.

Stirring Spoon

A large stirring spoon is needed to stir the beer in the boiling kettle and fermenter. Stainless steel or plastic spoons are preferable to the more aesthetic wooden ones, as wood is porous and therefore hard to sterilize.

Straining Bags

The small muslin 'hop bags' sold at home brewing stores are very useful for holding small amounts of grain for steeping before the boil, and for holding whole hops in the boiling wort. A strainer is usually not needed when pouring the cooled wort from the boiling pot to the fermenter, as pelletized hops will have settled to the bottom of the pot during the cooling process, and will be largely left behind when pouring or siphoning into the fermenter. A large colander or large straining bag is needed during transferring, however, when whole hops have been boiled in the wort.

Fermenters

After boiling the malt and hops, the finished wort is poured or siphoned into a fermenter, where yeast is added to ferment the raw sugary wort into alcoholic beer. A fermenter must be easy to clean and sterilize, and have an airtight closure fitted with an airlock, to release the fermentation-produced CO_2 gas while sealing out bacteria-laden outside air. Fermenters are usually of 6 to 7 gallon capacity (to hold 5 gallons of beer with room for fermentation-produced foaming).

The most commonly-sold style of fermenter is simply a six gallon or larger plastic bucket or drum with a removable airtight lid and airlock. A small valve is often installed near the bottom, so beer can be easily transferred without siphoning. If your fermenter is equipped with a valve, be sure to clean and sterilize the valve thoroughly after each batch, as beer spoiling bacteria can hide in its inner recesses.

Six to seven and one half gallon glass bottles (called carboys) sealed with a rubber bung and airlock are also popular as fermenters. Glass has the advantage of being completely non-porous and transparent, allowing thorough sterilization of the fermenter surface, and a good view of the turbulent fermentation process. Glass is more labor intensive than plastic as a siphon must be used to get the beer out, and handling and cleaning is a bit awkward. Home brewing stores sell L shaped brushes specifically designed for cleaning the difficult to reach inner shoulders of glass carboys.

Fermenter

Priming Container

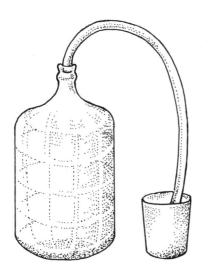

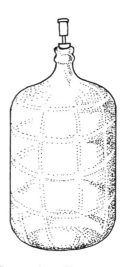

Blow-off Fermenter

Secondary Fermenter

A variation of the glass carboy fermenter is the blow-off fermenter, consisting of a 5 gallon glass water bottle with a 1" inner diameter vinyl hose stuck in its throat to seal the neck, which curves down and sits in a small bucket of sterilant solution, acting like a large airlock. As the blow-off fermenter is only 5 gallons in capacity and lacks headspace, the fermentation produced foaming has no where to go except to blow out through the 1" tube into the bucket of sterilant solution alongside the fermenter. The theory behind the blow off fermenter is that getting rid of the yeasty fermentation foam, instead of letting it fall back into the beer as with other fermenters, gives the beer a cleaner flavor. In reality, the flavor difference is hard to perceive between beers brewed in different fermenters. WARNING: The blow off fermenter can be dangerous and is therefore not recommended - if the hose is obstructed or plugged, a glass shrapnel laced explosion can result, possibly causing personal injury.

In hot weather or when brewing very light flavored, delicate beers, it is advantageous to transfer the beer from the fermenter into a secondary fermenter, to get the raw beer off the yeast sediment in the first fermenter. This yeasty sediment in the first (primary) fermenter can break down after the bulk of fermentation has ceased, releasing yeasty or bitter off-flavors into the beer. A secondary fermenter is usually a 5 gallon glass water bottle sealed with an airlock, although any clean, sterilized fermenter with an airlock will work.

Priming Container

After the beer has fermented out and is ready to bottle, a small amount of fermentable sugar must be stirred in right before bottling to give the yeast sufficient food to create carbonating gas in the bottle. A priming container is just a food grade 5 or 6 gallon container into which the beer can be transferred from the primary or secondary fermenter before bottling, so priming sugar can be stirred in without kicking up silty yeast sediment. Some priming containers feature bottling valves, so primed beer can be bottled without siphoning.

Transfer Tubing

To avoid aeration (which can cause oxidation and off-flavors), beer should never be 'splashed' before bottling. Transfer tubing (also used for siphoning) should be ⅜" in interior diameter and made of an easily cleanable material, such as clear vinyl. When siphoning, one must always avoid sucking up the yeast sediment on the bottom of the fermenter, so keep the tip of the hose at least 1 ½" above the bottom of the fermenter. Home brewing stores stock siphons specifically designed for sediment avoidance, or you can avoid siphoning by using a fermenter and priming container with draining valves installed.

Thermometer

A submersible thermometer is helpful for determining when to add the yeast and to monitor the temperature of your beer or brewing area. Exposed bulb instruments, like the old fashioned dairy type, or modern electronic models with waterproof probes, are best.

The Hydrometer

Unfermented wort is heavier (and denser) than fermented beer, because malt sugar is heavier than the alcohol it fosters. The hydrometer, a weighted glass float with a slender calibrated stem, measures how much heavier beer is than water, displaying the density where the stem emerges from the beer. The higher the density (the more malt in solution) the higher the hydrometer floats and the higher

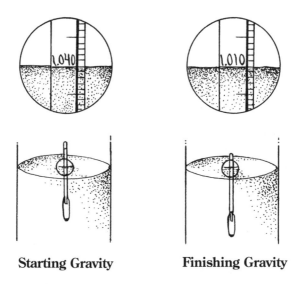

Starting Gravity   **Finishing Gravity**

the reading. As the yeast eats the sugar compounds in the raw beer, converting them to alcohol and carbon dioxide, the weight of the beer actually decreases, until all the sugar has been consumed and fermentation ceases.

Hydrometers calibrated with the specific gravity scale are used by home brewers in the United States, Canada, and England, primarily to find the starting gravity (initial strength) and to determine when the beer has finished fermenting and is ready for bottling. The specific gravity scale measures the progress of fermentation; as fermentation proceeds, the specific gravity reading drops. For simplicity, the specific gravity scale is often abbreviated by dropping the first two constant number (1.040 to 40).

Starting and finishing gravities vary widely depending on the amount and quality of malt, grain, yeast, and sugar used. Finishing gravities of all-malt beers end up higher (1.008 to 1.026) than those made with large amounts of sugar (1.000

to 1.007) as malt contains non-fermentables which remain after fermentation, increasing the weight and body of beer.

To take a reading, sterilize the hydrometer and place in the fermenter, spinning to dislodge any air bubbles that cling to the body of the instrument. The correct reading is at the point level with the surface of the beer, not the lower reading obtained where the beer bends up to embrace the slender glass stem.

Virtually all hydrometers are calibrated to give accurate readings at 60 degrees F., plus or minus 5 degrees. At 70 degrees, the instrument will read 1 degree too low because beer is less dense when warm. At 80 degrees, the hydrometer will read 2 degrees too low. And at 90 degrees, you will have to add 4½ degrees to the apparent reading to obtain the correct figure. Example: the hydrometer reads 1.038 at 80 degrees, though the correct temperature compensated reading is 1.040.

The hydrometer is employed twice while brewing: to determine the starting gravity, a good indication of the potential alcoholic strength of the beer, and later when the beer has finished fermenting, to determine if the beer has reached finished gravity and is safe to bottle.

To find the starting gravity, the first reading is taken after the unfermented beer (wort) has cooled and before the yeast is added. The second reading should be taken after the beer has fermented for at least 7 days and the airlock has stopped bubbling to determine if the finishing gravity has been reached. If the recipe is experimental and the finishing gravity is not known, one must take 2 readings three days apart to make sure the beer has finished fermenting (and the hydrometer has stopped dropping). Unless you thrill to the thought of beer bottles exploding like time-delay shrapnel bombs in your basement, bottle only when you are positive the hydrometer has stopped dropping.

Bottles

You will need 48 sterilized non-twist cap 12 ounce bottles or equivalent to hold a 5 gallon batch. The bottles should be strong (designed for beer or soda use) to hold the carbonation that builds after capping. Dark colored amber or green bottles are best, because they help keep damaging light from the aging beer. Do not use twist-cap bottles, because they are made of thin glass and are difficult to reseal.

Deposit 'bar bottles' (often called longnecks) are excellent for home brewing. Most imported beers also come in excellent bottles. Particularly good are the larger bottles with the recloseable ceramic stoppers, which eliminate the need for a bottle cap. Home brewing stores often have replacement gaskets for ceramic top bottles.

North American champagne bottles will accept a bottle cap, and being extremely strong, make excellent beer bottles. Another advantage is their 25 oz. size, which reduces work and bottle cap use by fifty percent.

Bottle Preparation

Beer bottles must be kept clean. The best way to keep bottles from getting dirty on the inside is to rinse them out with water shortly after the beer has been emptied. This is especially important with bottles containing home brewed beer, as the yeast sediment will provide food for tenacious mold growth if not rinsed out.

To thoroughly clean dirty beer bottles (and even remove most beer labels without scrubbing), soak them in a solution of TSP (Tri-Sodium-Phosphate) and diluted unscented laundry bleach. TSP is a common household cleaner available at hardware and paint stores. To make a working solution, add 3 level tablespoons to 1 gallon of water. Add 1 tablespoon of unscented household laundry bleach to this gallon mix to sterilize the bottles. Once you have your TSP/bleach solution, soak the beer bottles for 48 hours to remove all mold deposits and loosen labels. Rinse with water to remove all solution traces before filling with beer. TSP is hazardous, be sure to follow the safety instructions on the box, and wear eye protection and gloves when mixing.

Once your bottles have been cleaned with TSP, they can be kept clean for many uses by rinsing them immediately after emptying, and then sterilizing with diluted bleach sterilant (followed with a water rinse) before filling. Home brewing stores have many devices to aid in the cleaning and storing of bottles.

Bottle Capper

A quality bottle capper is a must for frustration free bottling. Get a good double lever or bench capper; a poorly made capper will make bottling an ordeal. Never use too much force when applying bottle caps, as even a good capper can break bottles if misused.

3 Ingredients

Grain

Any recognizable beer is based on malted barley and or malted wheat; barley or wheat kept moist until it sprouts, then kiln dried. To produce a darker beer with a caramelized or roasted malt flavor, some malted barley is kilned to varying degrees of darkness.

Before malted barley grain can be used for brewing, it must be crushed or ground, breaking the barrier-like husk to allow brewing water to dissolve the sweet malt flavors inside. Malted barley grain can often be purchased already crushed or ground at home brewing supply stores, or you can use a grain mill, rolling pin, or blender to crack the husks. Avoid pulverizing the grain into powder, as the resultant wet flour will make straining difficult.

The lightest grain, pale malted barley, is kilned lightly (just enough to dry) and produces the most sugar compounds when mashed. Whether mashed to convert its starches to fermentable sugars, or used in pre-mashed extract form (as described in this book), pale malted barley is the primary ingredient in all beers, light and dark, providing the majority of fermentable sugars. Closely related to pale malted barley is dextrin malt, which includes a high proportion of bodybuilding unfermentable dextrins, and Vienna and Munich malts, which are roasted at a slightly higher temperature to add a golden color and light nut-like flavor.

Like malted barley, malted wheat is kilned lightly, and used in the production of wheat beers. Malted wheat imparts a softer, more bread-like character to beer than the crisper flavored malted barley.

Crystal malt, known to commercial brewers as caramel malt, is malted barley subjected to higher oven temperatures which brown the barley like heat browns toast. Unlike pale malted barley, composed largely of starch, the starch in crystal malt is largely converted to fermentable sugars by a unique kilning process. Crystal malt is actually mashed in the kiln, at 150 to 170 degrees for up to 2 hours with a quantity of water, so that 'stewing' occurs and the starches in the malt convert into caramelized sugars. Crystal malt is kilned to varying degrees of darkness, and is often available in light as well as the usual amber form at home brewing stores. As the starches in crystal malt have already been converted to flavorful caramelized sugars, crystal malt is a very useful adjunct for the malt extract brewer who wants to modify the flavor of a malt extract without the work of mashing.

Chocolate malt is pale malted barley that has been roasted at 420 degrees F. until it turns the color of chocolate. Unlike crystal malt, chocolate malt has not been 'stewed', and does not contain fermentable sugars. Chocolate malt imparts its roasted malt flavor when steeped, and accordingly is a useful adjunct for the malt extract brewer.

Black patent malt is similar to Chocolate, only roasted at 450 degrees, until it turns black like espresso coffee. Like a darker roasted chocolate malt, black patent adds a black color and sweet roasted flavor when steeped.

Roasted barley is kilned in the same way as black patent, only it is prepared from unmalted barley instead of pale malted barley. As it is produced from unmalted barley, roasted barley has a drier, sharper character than black patent, and is very useful in the production of dry stout.

Unlike lighter roasted malts, chocolate, black patent, and roasted barley impart compounds which increase the surface tension of the finished beer, resulting in enhanced head retention.

Malt Extract

To produce extract for fermentation, crushed pale malted barley (sometimes mixed with crushed wheat malt for wheat beer) is mixed with water to a porridge-like consistency, and heated to 150 - 155 degrees F. for 1 to 2 hours in a process known as mashing, converting the starch compounds in the malt by enzyme activity into fermentable sugars. After mashing is complete, the sugary malt extract must be rinsed from the grain husks with hot water in a process called sparging. The extracted sweet fluid is then boiled with the hops to create raw unfermented beer, known in brewing circles as wort (pronounced 'wert'). Although some home brewers, seeking full control over their beers color and malt flavor, mash their own malt, most prefer to bypass the lengthy mashing process by using malt extract.

For the convenience of brewers who do not relish the prospect of spending 5 hours to make 5 gallons of beer, syrup and dry malt extracts are produced by evaporating water from freshly-mashed worts. Malt extracts for home brewing are all made without preservatives because chemical additives would kill the yeast and prevent fermentation.

19

Although most malt extracts are unhopped, some include hop flavor. The finest hopped malt extracts are hopped by boiling the wort with real hops before concentration, instead of merely hop flavored by the addition of hop extract. The advantage of hopped malt extract is its convenience, as the brewer does not need to add hops: the disadvantage is the brewer has less control over the final flavor of the beer, as bitterness level and hop variety are rarely given.

Malt extract is most commonly available in a syrup form, usually packaged in cans, pouches, or pails. Syrup malt extract is the least processed form of malt extract, and is available in wide variety of formulations, from very pale wheat extracts to coffee-black syrups made with roasted malts. Syrup malt extract typically contains 80% solids, making it 20% less strong per pound than dry malt extract, which contains 100% solids.

Dry malt extract is wort which has been completely dried for ease of handling. The sticky powder is more expensive than syrup malt, as it requires a greater amount of energy to produce, but has the advantage of ease of measurement, and is often used as a supplement to syrup malt extract.

Sugar and Adjuncts

In all-malt beers, corn or cane sugar are used only to provide food for the yeast in the bottled beer, enabling it to produce carbonating carbon dioxide gas. Corn sugar is frequently used in combination with malt extract in economy beer kits as a malt stretcher to bolster alcoholic strength, but the resultant sugar beer has a malt flavor distorted by the cidery flavor of fermented sugar. This is especially true if the wort is composed of more than 20% corn sugar (1 pound of sugar per 4 pounds of malt extract). Beer can be brewed from worts composed of 50% sugar or more, although hard cider might be a more accurate name than beer, in terms of flavor, for the fermented result.

Corn sugar (also known as dextrose) contains 100% glucose and is the most popular sugar in home brewing, as it leaves a minimal taste in the beer and ferments quickly. Household cane sugar can be used, although it contains fructose, a more difficult to ferment sugar which must be broken down by the yeast before fermentation. This break down process tends to leave a 'hot' sharp flavor in the finished beer. Accordingly, most home brewers stick to more expensive, readily fermentable corn sugar.

Rice extract or syrup is like malt extract, only mashed from rice. It has the advantage of having the same fermentable sugar content (45 to 55% fermentable maltose sugar) as most malt extracts, which means it will not ferment completely like corn sugar and leave a thin, cidery flavor. Rice syrup gives the extract home brewer an easy way to produce light rice adjunct beers, without the need for cooking and mashing rice. Rice syrup imparts a very light, crisp flavor. Like syrup malt extract, rice syrup is also available in a more expensive (and easier to measure) dry form.

Brown sugar and even molasses can be used in small amounts (try using them instead of corn sugar for priming) to add unique flavors to strong dark beers.

Lactose is unfermentable milk sugar, used sparingly when residual sweetness is desired in the finished beer. Small quantities (4 ounces in 5 gallons) of lactose add a little body to beer while slightly sweetening the flavor. Larger quantities (sweeten to taste) are used when brewing English-style stout or sweet bock beers. Lactose can be added during the last few minutes of the boil in its dry state, or heated with water to make a sugar syrup and stirred in to taste before bottling. Beers containing lactose should not be served to people allergic to milk.

Dextrin powder is a composed of 94 to 98% unfermentable dextrins (derived from rice or corn), which can be stirred into boiling wort to increase the viscosity and apparent smoothness of beer. Dextrins are unfermentable compounds that remain after fermentation is finished; adding 1 to 6 ounces of dextrin powder during the wort boil (the fine gummy powder is hard to dissolve) will increase the thickness and fullness of the finished beer, although it makes beer harder to clear when aging.

Hops

Before the use of hops became commonplace in the 17th century, beer must of been an insipid beverage by todays standards, sweet and mild, without a trace of refreshing hop bitterness. Hops, originally added to beer for the bacteria-inhibiting qualities of their alpha acid, soon became essential in brewing, probably because their complex, refreshing bitterness is a perfect complement to sweet malt.

The alpha acid in hops provide the bitter flavor in beer and also give the wort a measure of protection, as alpha acid has the ability to retard the growth of bacteria with little effect on yeast growth. Alpha acid also provides an approximate measurement of the bittering value of hops per ounce; the higher the alpha acid, the greater the bittering. Keep in mind, however, that every variety of hop has a differently perceived bitter flavor, and a Kent Golding with a 5% alpha acid content has a spicy, woody bitterness, while a Cascade with the identical alpha acid will have a floral, almost sweetly bitter, character.

Hops are loosely divided into flavoring and aromatic varieties, based on the amount of bittering alpha acids and the quality of the aromatic oils they contain. Hops noted for their fine aroma, like Hallertau and Tettnanger, may be low in bittering alpha acids, but possess volatile (aromatic) oils of refined, delicate aroma. Traditional flavoring hops, like Cluster and Bullion, possess higher levels of bittering acids, but their aromatic oils usually have a coarse aroma.

When choosing a hop, consider both the bitter flavor it imparts and its aroma. Most brewers use more than one variety in a beer, choosing hops that go well together, like a cook selects spices. Aroma in hops is easy to determine - smell a sample, and if you can picture the aroma in your beer, use the hop. Unlike aroma, the varying bitter flavor of hops is a bit more difficult to determine from a raw sample. If you lack experience, use the aroma as a clue; a hop like Hallertau with a spicy aroma will have a more spicy flavor than a hop like Cascade, whose floral aroma hints of its mild, almost sweet and fruity, bitter flavor.

The only part of the hop plant used in brewing is the female flower cone. The hop plant, a close relative of Cannabis Sativa, contains lupulin (a mild sedative) in its female flower cones. Most home brews, with a higher hopping rate than the average commercial beers, also have a more relaxing effect on the drinker, assuming the alcohol content is the same.

Hops are available in two forms, whole and pellet. Whole hops, though commonly available in less variety than pellet hops, are preferred by some brewers, as they are completely unprocessed. Whole hop flower cones may also help coagulate protein matter during the wort boil, the soggy cones providing many surfaces for the churning malt proteins to thrash against.

Whole Hops   **Pellet Hops**

Pellet hops are whole hops that have been pressed and extruded to resemble rabbit food. Artificial binding agents or other additives are not used in the production of pellet hops. Hops in pellet form have a longer shelf life than whole hops, as their compacted form helps protect the delicate hop oils from air contact. In addition, hops in pellet form are easier to measure, and do not need to be strained from the boil, as they settle out with the trub (coagulated wort proteins) when the wort is cooled.

It is important to use only fresh, properly stored hops. Ideally hops should be refrigerated, or at least packed in barrier bags (if you cannot smell the hops when you smell the bag, they are in barrier bags). Fresh hops have a rich aroma and a slight moisture content, evident in pellets and whole hops by a lack of brittle dryness. Poorly-stored faded hops, on the other hand, will have a faint or musty aroma, and be very dry.

It is also important to know the alpha acid content of the hops you are buying, as hops can vary 20% year to year in their alpha acid (bittering acid) content. Ideally, the alpha acid percentage will be printed on the bag, if not, ask your home brewing supplier for an alpha acid figure: they may be able to look it up for you.

Refrigerate your hops in sealed barrier bags or glass jars when you get home.

Bullion is a traditional coarse flavoring hop, ideal for stronger dark ales and stouts. Brewers Gold is a closely related variety that is almost out of production. Bullion alpha acid averages 7.5%.

Cascade is a very popular aromatic hop, with a low bitterness level and fragrant, flowery aroma. Cascade is the best example of a hop with a floral character. Alpha acid averages 4.5%.

Chinook is a new high alpha acid variety, with a wonderful smoky character. An excellent hop for ale brewers. Alpha acid averages 11%.

Cluster, used in many U.S. commercial beers, has an average bitterness and somewhat coarse aroma. A decent flavoring hop, but not generally used for finishing better beers. Alpha acid averages 7%.

East Kent Goldings are the premier English aromatic, unsurpassed for imparting a rich spicy character to ales. Usually expensive, but worth it for their unique refined character. Alpha acid averages 5%.

Fuggles are grown extensively in both England and the U.S., and have a mild woody flavor and clean full bitterness. English fuggles generally have a higher (4.5%) alpha acid content and more pronounced aroma than fuggles grown in Oregon, which are milder, with an average alpha acid of around 4%.

Hallertau is the premier European aromatic, used in many of the worlds finest lagers. Hallertau has a refined, spicy aroma and mild full bitterness. Alpha acid content averages around 4%, but ranges quite a bit from crop to crop.

Mount Hood is a new aromatic hop grown in the U.S., with a unique character, like a cross between a spicy Hallertau and floral Cascade. Excellent as a finishing hop in lagers and ales. Alpha acid can range from 3.5% to over 6%, as this hop has been in limited production.

Northern Brewer has a unique woody character, with a flavor reminiscent of evergreen trees and mint. An aggressive hop, traditionally used in steam-style beer and stronger ales. Alpha acid averages 7%.

Perle is a new variety, with a flavor like a cross between Northern Brewer and Cascade. Perle has a slightly more refined flavor and a more floral aroma than Northern Brewer. Alpha acid averages 7%.

Saaz is the famous spicy pilsner hop from Czechoslovakia, used in the production of Pilsner Urquell. An excellent lager hop, Saaz has a rich spicy flavor and aroma. Alpha acid averages 5%.

Styrians are like a cross between Saaz and Fuggle, with a refined smooth flavor. An excellent, underrated hop for both lagers and ales. Alpha acid averages 6%.

Tettnanger is a subtle hop with a soft character, that blends beautifully with malt and wheat flavors in lighter beers. Excellent for wheat beers and light lagers. Alpha acid averages 4.0%.

Willamette is a new fuggle variant, with a smooth soft flavor and mild, almost sweet, aroma. Alpha acid averages 4.0%.

Spices

Home brewers are increasingly using spices such as cinnamon, ginger, nutmeg, and cloves to add unique flavors to holiday brews. Spices should be added when the heat is turned off at the end of the boil, and allowed to steep as the wort cools. Spices should be in chopped or powdered form for adding to wort. It is easy to add too much spice flavor: use no more than ¼ ounce per 5 gallons when trying spices for the first time.

Oak Chips

Perhaps most authentic in India pale ale, oak adds a rich complexity to beer, joining with hop flavor to add a spicy balance to the sweet malt. To impart an oak character, use 1 to 4 ounces of oak chips (available at wine and brewing supply stores) per 5 gallons. Oak chips should be steam sterilized in a vegetable cooker for 20 minutes, and added to beer in a secondary fermenter. When the oak chips sink to the bottom in about 8 days, the beer is ready to bottle. Do not reuse oak chips, as they are hard to sterilize after being soaked with yeast.

Yeast

Without the lowly yeast, no alcoholic beverages could exist. Yeast is a fungus which feeds on sugar compounds in beer, converting them to alcohol, carbon dioxide, and flavor compounds. Though often taken for granted, yeast has an enormous influence on beer flavor, as every drop of beer passes through a yeast cell during fermentation. The strain (variety) of yeast used, and its purity, greatly affect the flavor of the finished beer. Differing strains can impart flavors ranging from dry to sweet, spicy or mild, and affect the body of the beer by attenuating the wort to varying final gravities. The purity of the yeast is most important, as yeast infected with even a very small amount of bacteria or wild yeast (as found in some dried home brewing yeasts) will add a yeasty or somewhat sour-cidery flavor. Yeast is available in two forms, liquid and dry. Liquid yeast, though expensive and delicate, is often purer than dry yeast, and is currently available in more strains than dry yeast, giving you more control over beer flavor. Liquid yeast is commonly available in a self-starting pack, and must be started one or two days in advance of brewing. Liquid yeast is very perishable and should be stored in a refrigerator prior to use.

Dry yeast is the most popular form of yeast for home brewing. Dry yeast can be prepared 15 minutes before use, and is generally less costly than the more fussy liquid yeast. Besides its ease of use, dry brewing yeast has the great advantage of being very durable, as it is able to survive higher and lower temperatures (refrigeration is not required) than perishable liquid yeast.

Although the home brewing trade has increasingly offered improved strains of dried brewing yeast, some have been produced quickly and cheaply in bread yeast plants, and the resultant yeast is often contaminated with trace amounts of bacteria and wild yeast, impossible to avoid in an industrial environment. Fortunately, new improved (and more costly) strains of dried brewing yeast are becoming available, which are well worth the extra cost. Yeast can also be started from commercial bottles of beer that contain a yeast sediment, as long as the beer is not too old or pasteurized (see chapter 9). Ask your home brewing supplier for their recommendation on a good dried or liquid brewing yeast, keeping in mind that a little extra spent on yeast can prevent off-flavors in the finished beer.

Yeast strains are loosely divided into two basic types, top-fermenting and bottom-fermenting. Top fermenting beer yeast, commonly known as ale yeast, performs the bulk of its work on the surface of the beer (it is more prone to floating), and is traditionally used to make ale, stout, porter, and some wheat beers. Ale yeast works best at temperatures between 60 and 65 degrees F. Used to make lager and steam-style beer, bottom-fermenting lager yeast works largely on the floor of the fermenter, and prefers a slightly cooler fermentation temperature, ideally 55 to 60 degrees F.

For fermenting potent barley-wine beers with starting gravities in excess of 1.080, alcohol-resistant champagne yeast is often used, as ale or lager yeast can become pickled in alcohol, resulting in stuck fermentations, when working such strong beers. Champagne yeast imparts a vinous character, and works best at 60 to 65 degrees F.

Brewing Water

The water used for brewing should have a neutral taste and be free of excessive chlorine and odors. Any off-taste in the water will carry over to the finished beer. Excessive chlorine (if you can smell it, it is excessive) can be removed by boiling prior to brewing for 45 minutes. Bottled water should be used if the local tap water is tainted.

Most tap water in North America has a hardness level of 70 to 200 parts per million (PPM). Ideally, brewing water should have a hardness of at least 200 PPM, as harder water encourages the coagulation and subsequent settling of proteins in the wort boil. Adding a teaspoon of food grade gypsum will raise the water hardness of 5 gallons by approximately 165 PPM, and is recommended unless you know your water is very hard. Call your water company for a PPM hardness figure, or test your water with water hardness test strips.

4 The Brewing Process

After the sweet wort has been reconstituted from malt extract, it must be boiled for 1 hour with hops for flavoring, protein removal, and sterilization. The finished wort is then cooled and placed in a fermenter with yeast to begin fermentation, during which yeast eats the malt sugar, converting it to alcohol, carbon dioxide, and flavor compounds. After 7 days or more of fermentation, the beer must be primed with additional yeast food (usually corn sugar) and capped, to allow carbonation buildup and aging before drinking.

Brewing is as much an art of shaping as of mixing. Malt and hops are not merely combined in hot water to form wort, they are boiled violently for an hour, ridding the malt though collision and coagulation of its raw haze and off-flavor causing proteins, and evaporating excessive aromatic hop oils while converting insoluble hop alpha acids into dissolved hop flavor. Like a lengthy slow simmer develops the flavor and texture of a delicate sauce, a vigorous boil shapes the flavor and polishes the look of beer.

At the start of the 1 hour boil, the initial flavoring hops are added to provide bittering. After 30 minutes, a second charge of flavoring hops is sometimes added, to provide both bittering and a deeper hop flavor, as hop flavor (not to be confused with hop bitterness) is partially boiled away after 40 minutes of boiling.

1. Boiling

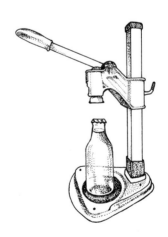

2. Fermentation

3. Priming

4. Bottling

After 55 minutes, right before the end of the boil, aromatic hops are usually added, as the volatile aromatic hop oils in the flavoring hops added earlier have wafted free of the hot tossing wort.

For the ultimate in efficient boils, 5 gallons of water should be boiled with the malt and hops when making 5 gallons of beer. For those with only a 4 or 5 gallon pot, however, a decent boil can still be obtained with 3 gallons of water, although the danger of a sticky boil over of the more concentrated malt solution is greater. In addition, more concentrated boils tend to darken the color of the finished beer, because more sugary malt comes in contact with the hot pot surface.

After boiling, the wort should be cooled as rapidly as possible to 85 degrees F. or less. Rapid cooling helps settle out the flock-like protein 'trub' coagulated during the one hour boil, and also minimizes the time before the yeast can be safely added (which starts fermentation), reducing the risk of bacterial infection in the vulnerable, non-fermenting wort. Cooling can be accelerated by putting the boiling pot in a sink of cold water or by using a specially designed wort chiller.

When cool, the wort is siphoned or poured carefully off the coagulated protein and hop sediment (brewers call it trub) into a sterilized fermenter, where yeast (and cold water if necessary to make 5 gallons) is added and fermentation begins. During the first vigorous stage of fermentation, a large amount of carbon dioxide is produced, giving rise to a foam head on the surface of the brew. After 2 or 3 days, the foaming subsides and the beer continues to ferment and settle for about 7 more days.

After fermentation has ceased, the beer is checked with a hydrometer to be sure a reasonable finished gravity has been reached, and the beer is safe to bottle. This is done because bottling while the beer is still fermenting is dangerous, and can lead to exploding bottles.

The fermented beer is alcoholic and flat. Immediately before bottling, a process known as priming, which evokes a gentle renewed fermentation from the yeast still in suspension, is employed; a small amount of corn sugar (usually 4 to 4½ oz.) is stirred into the 5 gallons of beer, giving the yeast more food to digest into carbon dioxide and alcohol. As this fermentation occurs after the beer is bottled and capped, the carbon dioxide pressure carbonates the brew instead of escaping. Priming adds a bit less than ¼% of alcohol to the finished beer.

After priming and capping, beer is aged according to type. Ales, porters, and stouts are aged at fermentation temperature for 2 to 4 weeks before drinking, while lagers (lager is a German word meaning 'to store') are aged at fermentation temperature for 6 days to facilitate carbonation, and then refrigerated until they become sparklingly clear in 4 to 7 weeks.

5 What Style of Beer?

There are three basic types of beers; ales, brewed at warmer temperatures with top-fermenting ale yeast, lagers, brewed at cooler temperatures (and aged under refrigeration) using bottom-fermenting lager yeast, and steam-style beers, which are lagers brewed at warmer ale temperatures. Keep in mind that the brewing and aging method have a greater effect on the type of beer produced than the type of yeast used. For example, a steam-style beer brewed with bottom-fermenting lager yeast but produced and aged at warmer ale temperatures tastes more like an ale than a lager.

Ale, brewed with the more forgiving top-fermenting ale yeast, usually has a stronger flavor than lager. Like steam-style beer, ale is usually easier for the first time brewer, because fermentation and aging can be carried out at room temperature (ideally 60 to 65 degrees F.).

Steam-style beer is lager brewed at ale temperatures. Developed in San Francisco in the 1900's by Eastern brewers desiring lager but lacking refrigeration, steam has a hearty flavor, imparted by both the traditional high hopping rate and flavor compounds produced by lager yeast at warmer brewing temperatures. The word steam, when used in commerical brewing, is now a trademark of Anchor Brewing Company in San Francisco.

Like steam-style beer, lager beer is brewed with bottom-fermenting lager yeast. Lager has a smoother, less pronounced flavor than ale or steam because it is brewed at cooler temperatures and aged under refrigeration for at least a month before drinking. Lager is the most difficult beer for the home brewer, as fermentation temperatures should be kept at 70 degrees F. or lower, and refrigerated aging is required for at least 4 weeks after capping to develop the smooth and mellow lager flavor.

Temperature

Whether you brew a true ale, steam, or lager beer depends largely on the temperature of your fermentation and aging areas. Ale is the most forgiving, and can be brewed at temperatures ranging from 55 to 80 degrees F., steam-style from 55 to 75 degrees, and lager from 50 to 70 degrees. The optimum temperature for ale and steam beer is a steady 60 to 65 degrees: for lager, a steady 55 to 60 degrees.

Temperatures warmer than optimum will produce stronger flavored beers, as the yeast will produce excessive off-flavor compounds (imparting a stronger, rougher flavor) while rapidly fermenting the overheated beer. Fermentation temperature should be steady (do not ferment outside or in an unheated shed) as temperature variations over 12 degrees in one day can shock yeast, causing it to release astringent flavors.

In hot weather, the fermenter can be cooled by 3 to 5 degrees (and buffered against large temperature variations) by placing it in a tub of water and wrapping with an absorbent wet towel. The evaporation of water from the wick-like towel cools the beer. For the ultimate in temperature control, some home brewing stores sell a refrigerator regulator that lets you turn an old refrigerator into a temperature controlled environment for fermentation and aging.

Aging

Like much in life, beer goes through a maturation period before reaching its prime. Ale and steam beer should be aged in a dark place indoors, ideally at a steady temperature of 55 to 65 degrees F. Ale and steam-style beer with starting gravities of 1.055 or less will be quite good 2 weeks after bottling, and reach peak flavor in 3 to 4 weeks. Stronger beers with higher gravities should be aged at least 3 weeks before drinking.

True lager beer is aged under refrigeration; 'lager' aged at room temperature is steam beer. To produce a true lager, bottle and store at fermentation temperature for 6 days to facilitate the carbonation process, then refrigerate until the beer becomes sparklingly clear, usually in 4 to 7 weeks, before drinking.

For the finest beer, age according to type: lager under refrigeration, and ale and steam beer at room temperature. All beers should be aged in a dark area, to prevent light reactions with hop compounds (producing a 'skunky' flavor) and the aging temperature, whether cold or room temperature, should be steady.

6 Recipe Design

Much of the pleasure and satisfaction derived from home brewing comes from being able to design your own beer. The basic recipes in the next chapter are intended to be guidelines, rather than commandments etched in stone: after you gain experience, feel free to alter them to suit your own taste.

Malt provides sweetness and alcoholic strength, hops the balancing bitterness. If you desire a sweeter beer, either add more malt or cut back on the hops. Conversely, to reduce sweetness, add more hops or cut back on the malt used. Whatever modification you make from batch to batch, it is vital to write it down, so you can trace the flavor changes to the recipe.

Starting Gravity

Starting gravities for light refreshing beers can be as low as 1.030 and as high as 1.090 for potent barley wines. To determine the approximate starting gravity of your own recipe, add up the total degrees of extract (see the chart on page 62) of all the pounds of extract producing ingredients included, and divide by the number of gallons you intend to brew. For example, a 5 gallon recipe calling for 6 lbs. of syrup malt extract (34 degrees per pound, multiplied by 6) and ½ pound of crushed crystal grain (16 degrees per pound, divided by 2) has a total of 212 degrees of extract, which, when divided by 5 (gallons), yields an approximate starting gravity of 1.042.

Finishing Gravity

Unlike starting gravities, finishing gravities are difficult to calculate with a reasonable degree of accuracy, because different malt extracts contain varying amounts of unfermentables, and some yeast strains eagerly consume malt sugars others find unpalatable. Although impossible to calculate precisely, a rough rule of thumb can be given to help establish some idea of the approximate finishing gravity of an all-malt beer. Divide the starting gravity of the beer by 3.7 (drop the first two constant numbers: 1.042 to 42 before dividing). For example, an all malt beer with a starting gravity of 1.042 (42), when divided by 3.7, has an estimated finishing gravity of 1.011 (11). As this calculated finishing gravity can be as much as 20% higher or lower than the actual final gravity, depending on the ingredients used and fermentation conditions, it is useful only as a rough guide. Taking two readings with the hydrometer three days apart before bottling is still necessary to be certain the beer's specific gravity has stopped dropping and it is safe to bottle.

Alcohol Content

The alcohol content of beer is determined by the amount of fermentable sugar compounds available for the yeast to consume in the freshly-cooled wort prior to fermentation. The higher the fermentable sugar level, the higher the alcohol content of the finished beer. To determine the approximate alcohol content of your finished beer by volume, subtract the finishing gravity from the starting gravity (dropping the first two constant numbers: 1.042 to 42), and multiply the resulting gravity drop by .129.

For example, a beer with a starting gravity of 1.042 (42) and a finishing gravity of 1.011 (11) has a gravity drop of 31, which, when multiplied by .129, results in an approximate alcohol content of 4% by volume.

Calculating Hop Bitterness

Like a cook without spices, a brewer would be lost without hops. Hops provide the refreshing bitterness needed to balance the sweet malt in beer. Like the cook, the brewer learns from experience how much hop flavor is needed to balance beer: too little, and the beer is bland, too much, and the delicate malt flavor is overwhelmed by penetrating bitterness.

As in cooking, a balanced flavor is vital. We have all probably tasted the too-bitter first efforts of overly enthusiastic beginners, as well as bland commercial products, produced by those whose market share depends on not offending anyone. Home brewers have traditionally used quite high hopping levels, probably at least partially to mask infected yeast or heat-wave induced flavor defects. With the widespread availability of improved yeast strains and temperature control (ranging from simple water baths to thermostat-supplemented refrigerators), home brewers can finally concentrate on the fine art of balancing their beer's bitter flavor.

The flavor balance of beer is largely established in the wort boil, where hops are added to the malt solution and boiled to dissolve and extract their bitter flavor into the beer. To easily calculate the amount of alpha acid added to a beer, Dave Line (author of the Big Book of Brewing) devised a simple system of Alpha Acid Units (AAU's) in the early seventies, which is still in use today. One alpha acid unit is the amount of acid contained in 1 oz. of 1% alpha acid hops. Accordingly, two ounces of Cascade with an alpha acid rating of 5%   (2 * 5) has a total of 10 AAU's, while 1 ½ oz. of Perle with an alpha acid rating of 7.0%   (1.5 * 7)   has a total of 10.5 AAU's.

Alpha acid units are a valuable guide in producing balanced beers   because they allow for adjustment in hopping level when using different alpha acid content hops. This is vital, as the same variety of hop can vary 20%   or more each crop in alpha acid content, depending on the weather and soil conditions. For example, if a recipe calls for 12 AAU's using 3 oz. of 4%   alpha acid English Fuggle hops in a 5 gallon batch, and all you have are 5.6% alpha East Kent Golding hops, just divide the recipe's 12 AAU's by your hops alpha rating (5.6) to get 2.14 oz., the amount of 5.6% alpha hops required to replicate the bitterness of 3 oz. of 4%   alpha hops in 5 gallons.

Though a great guide, alpha acid units do not give a clue as to how well the raw alpha acid added to the beer has been isomerized (transformed by heat) into flavorful iso-alpha acids. The insoluble alpha acid in hops is what eventually imparts the bitterness, after it is transformed through the hot abuse of boiling into   iso-alpha acids, which provide a clean bitter flavor. Raw hop alpha acid is only slightly soluble in cold beer and has little if any flavor; the boil-converted iso-alpha acids, on the other hand,   dissolve readily in beer and provide a clean bitterness. In a vigorous, dilute wort boil, it takes 50 minutes for raw hop alpha acids to be adequately converted to flavorful iso-alpha acids.   Aromatic hops, added during the last 5 minutes or by dry hopping, add only a slight   level of bitterness because their alpha acids are not heated long enough to convert them to soluble iso-alpha acids. In the most efficient of boils   (hops added at the beginning of a 1 hour dilute rolling boil) 30%   of the alpha acid is converted into flavor-producing iso-alpha acids.

This isomerization, or converting of raw hop alpha acid into soluble and flavorful iso-alpha acids, governed by time and temperature, is also influenced by the density of the wort and the form of hops used. Highly concentrated extract worts, say a 5 gallon malt extract batch brewed in two gallons of water, are less efficient in converting the insoluble hop alpha acids into dissolvable iso-alpha acids than more dilute worts. Pelletized hops are more easily isomerized than whole hops, as their particles disperse readily in the boil.

International Bittering Units

Knowing the degree of utilization of hop bitterness is important if we want to reasonably calculate our beers International Bittering Units (IBU's). International Bittering Units are a worldwide standard of bitterness measurement, valuable to home brewers as a way of comparing the hop bitterness level of home brew with that of commercial beers.

To calculate IBU's from per gallon AAU's, first determine the approximate efficiency of hop isomerization. Assuming the use of pellet hops, a dilute 3-5 gallon boil of average gravity (1.038 - 1.048), pellet hops boiled for 50 to 60 minutes will have 30% of their alpha acids converted to bittering iso-alpha acids. Pellet hops boiled for 30 minutes will have 21% of their alpha acids converted, while aromatic pellet hops boiled for 5 minutes (but steeped in 150 degree or hotter wort for 20 to 30 minutes during cooling) will have 10% of their alpha acids transformed into noticeable bitterness. For less readily isomerized whole hops, subtract 15% from the above conversion percentages.

To find your hop isomerization percentage, figure the percent isomerization of each of your hop additions. For example, if you add 1 oz. of 5% alpha hops (5 AAU's) at the beginning of the boil, ½ oz. of 4% alpha hops (2 AAU's) after 30 minutes, and ½ oz. of 3% alpha hops (1.5 AAU's) after 55 minutes, you have the following:

First Flavoring: 5 AAU'S times .30 (30% conversion) = 1.5 AAU's
Second Flavoring: 2 AAU's times .21 (21% conversion) = .42 AAU's
Aromatic hops: 1.5 AAU's times .10 (10% conversion) = .15 AAU's"

8.5 raw AAU's before the boil
2.07 isomerized AAU's after the boil
24% conversion of alpha to iso-alpha acids

Divide 2.07 (converted iso-alpha) by the number of gallons (5) to get .414, the amount of iso-alpha acids per gallon of finished beer.

To convert to International Bittering Units, divide the final isomerized alpha acid units (.414) by the amount of iso-alpha acids in one IBU (.01335) to get 31, the approximate number of IBU's in one gallon of your finished beer.

Registered Trademark	IBU's
Budweiser O.G. 1.044	.12
Spaten Club Weiss O.G. 1.050	.14
Beck's Light O.G. 1.044	.23
Anchor Steam O.G. 1.050	.40
Pilsner Urquell O.G. 1.048	.43
Red Tail Ale O.G. 1.055	.45
Guinness Stout O.G. 1.050	.50

When comparing the above commercial beers, keep in mind that malt provides sweetness to offset bitterness. Accordingly, the original gravity (O.G.) must be matched to achieve the same bitterness balance.

7 Recipes

The recipes included are generic, without malt or yeast brand names. Consider them guidelines to basic beer styles, adaptable to both your local ingredients and whims. All recipes are for 5 gallons.

Malt Extract

Malt extract is specified by color, and occasionally country of origin, as different countries have different barleys that impart unique flavors. Only unhopped malt extracts should be used, as it is impossible to fully control a recipe when you do not know how much hop flavor has been added in advance. It is important to purchase fresh malt extract of good quality, as poor quality malt can add a caramelized or biscuit-like tang to beer. If you are using the popular 3.3 lb. cans of unhopped malt extract, using two to get 6.6 lbs. is acceptably close to the 6 lbs. specified in many recipes.

Hops and AAU's

The recipes are for pelletized hops; if you use whole hops, use 15% more by weight. Alpha acid units are given, to help you balance your beer with changing hop alpha acid levels (see the previous chapter). If you know the alpha acid percentage of your hops, this will enable you to precisely match the recipes bitterness level, or use other varieties of dif-

ferent alpha acid content. If the alpha acid content is un-
known, simply follow the hop varieties and weights listed for
a close match.

To determine the alpha acid units in a given amount of hops,
multiply the weight by the alpha acid level. For example, if
you have 2 oz. of 4.5% alpha acid Cascade, multiply 2 * 4.5
to get 9, the number of Alpha acid units (AAU's) in the 2 oz.
of Cascade.

Conversely, to determine how many hops containing 4.2%
alpha acid you will need to match 12 AAU's, divide the
alpha acid units (12) by 4.2 to get 2.85, the weight in ounces
of 4.2% alpha acid hops needed to achieve 12 AAU's.

Yeast

To produce a clean flavor, it is vital to use good quality
brewing yeast. Though more costly and delicate, liquid
yeast cultures generally have a cleaner flavor than most dry
yeasts, although some excellent dry yeasts, particularly top
fermenting ale strains, are now available.

Ask your home brewing supplier about the best yeasts currently on the market, and remember that it does not pay to
save a few cents on yeast, when a poor quality strain could
make the entire batch sour.

Summer Beer

A light and thirst quenching beer for warmer weather. Ferment at room temperature like an ale. After bottling, let age at ferment temperature for 7 days to build carbonation, and then refrigerate as much of the batch as possible for 4 weeks, for a smooth lagered flavor.

    4 lbs. light malt extract
    2 lbs. rice extract or syrup
    First flavoring: ½ oz. Hallertau (2 AAU's)
    Second flavoring: ½ oz. Hallertau (2 AAU's)
    Aromatic: ¼ oz. Saaz hops (1.25 AAU's)
    1 teaspoon gypsum
    1 teaspoon Irish moss
    1 package dried ale yeast or liquid ale yeast starter
    4 ½ oz. corn sugar for carbonation

Starting gravity: 1.041, finishes at 1.012 or less.

Bitter

A very easy and rewarding lighter ale for the home brewer, bitter is best when fermented at 60 to 65 degrees F., and aged at 55 to 65 degrees for 2 to 3 weeks.

    6 lbs. light English malt extract
    First flavoring: 1 oz. Fuggle (4.5 AAU's)
    Second flavoring: ½ oz. Fuggle (2.2 AAU's)
    Aromatic: ½ oz. Golding (2.5 AAU's)
    1 teaspoon gypsum
    1 teaspoon Irish moss
    1 package dried ale yeast or liquid ale yeast starter
    4 oz. corn sugar for carbonation

Starting Gravity: 1.040, finishes at 1.013 or less.

Pale Ale

Stronger and more bitter in flavor than the curiously named bitter, pale ale has a dry malt base to bring out all the flavor and aroma of the best quality hops.

    6 lbs. light English malt extract syrup
    1 lb. light dry malt extract
    12 oz. crushed amber crystal malt (lovibond 40)
    First flavoring: 1¼ oz. Fuggle (5.6 AAU's)
    Second flavoring: 1½ oz. Fuggle (6.75 AAU's)
    Aromatic: ½ oz. Golding (2.5 AAU's)
    2 teaspoons gypsum
    1 teaspoon Irish moss
    1 package dried ale yeast or liquid ale yeast starter
    4 oz. corn sugar for carbonation

Starting gravity: 1.043, finishes at 1.014 or less.

Wheat Beer

A lightly hopped wheat beer in the style of the weizenbiers of southern Germany. Brew like an ale, and consume within 4 weeks of capping for the freshest flavor. For the most authentic flavor, try to get wheat malt extract that contains at least 50% wheat, and brew with liquid wheat beer yeast.

    6 lbs. wheat and barley malt extract (at least 50% wheat)
    First flavoring: 1 oz. Hallertau (4 AAU's)
    Second flavoring: none
    Aromatic: ½ oz. Hallertau or Cascade (2 AAU's)
    2 teaspoons gypsum
    1 teaspoon Irish moss
    1 package dried ale yeast or liquid wheat beer yeast starter
    4 ½ oz. corn sugar for carbonation

Starting gravity: 1.040, finishes at 1.012 or less.

Black Cherry Ale

A uniquely refreshing beer, with just enough hoppiness to temper the rich cherry flavors. The cherry juice adds a dusky rose color, and a rich fruity background to the traditional malt flavor. Best when brewed at ale temperatures, and then lagered for 2 months to mellow and blend the complex flavors. It is important to use as good a quality black cherry juice as you can; do not use juices containing added sugars or flavorings.

 6 ½ lbs. light malt extract
 3 quarts black cherry juice *
 First flavoring: 1 oz. Hallertau (4 AAU's)
 Second flavoring: none
 Aromatic: ¼ oz. Cascade (1 AAU)
 1 teaspoon Irish moss
 2 teaspoons gypsum
 1 package dried ale yeast or liquid ale yeast starter
 4 ½ oz. corn sugar for carbonation

*Add the black cherry juice at the end of the boil, when you turn off the heat.

Starting gravity: 1.049, finishes at 1.012 or less.

Porter

A great recipe, simple and almost foolproof. Like all ales, porter is an easy and rewarding beer to brew at home. Age 2 weeks before drinking.

6 lbs. dark Australian or English malt extract syrup
First flavoring: ½ oz. Northern Brewer or Perle (3.5 AAU's)
Second flavoring: ¾ oz. Northern Brewer or Perle (5.25 AAU's)
Aromatic: ¼ oz. Willamette or Fuggle (1 AAU)
1 teaspoon gypsum
1 teaspoon Irish moss
1 package dried ale yeast or liquid ale yeast starter
4 oz. corn sugar for carbonation

Starting gravity: 1.040, finishes at 1.012 or less.

Stout

Heavier than porter, with a more pronounced roasted malt flavor. Brew and age like an ale.

6 lbs. dark Australian or English malt extract syrup
1 ½ lbs. light dry malt extract
8 oz. crushed black patent, steeped before the boil
4 oz. crushed roasted barley, steeped before the boil
First flavoring: 1 ¼ oz. Perle or Northern Brewer (8.75 AAU's)
Second flavoring: ½ oz. Cascade or Fuggle (2 AAU's)
Aromatic: ¼ oz. Willamette or Fuggle (1 AAU)
2 teaspoons gypsum
1 teaspoon Irish moss
1 packet dried ale yeast or liquid ale yeast starter
4 oz. corn sugar for carbonation

Starting gravity: 1.055, finishes at 1.021 or less.

Barley Wine

Not a true wine, but an intense amber ale in the English tradition, well suited for sipping and savoring. Serve in a wine glass at 55 to 65 degrees F. to fully reveal the robust and vinous character.

Barley wine (also called Strong Ale) is fascinating to age as it changes noticeably through the months (and years). A few weeks after bottling, barley wine tastes rich, though a bit raw, with the malt and hop flavors separate and fresh. After six months, the flavors have blended, though the yeast sediment has decomposed, adding a new yeasty (and often bitter) flavor to the brew. After a year or more of cellar aging, the harsh yeasty flavors introduced by the dead yeast sediment mellow and blend, adding a new, almost smoky dimension to the more familiar malt and hop flavors.

> 12 lbs. light malt extract syrup
> 1 lb. crushed amber (40 lovibond) crystal malt
> First flavoring: 5 oz. Golding or English Fuggle (25 AAU's)
> Second flavoring: 1 ½ oz. Golding or English Fuggle (7.5 AAU's)
> Aromatic: 1 oz. Golding or English Fuggle (5 AAU's)
> 3 teaspoons gypsum
> 1 teaspoon Irish moss
> 2 packets dried champagne yeast, or liquid champagne yeast starter
> 3 ½ oz. corn sugar for carbonation

Starting gravity: 1.075, finishes at 1.026 or less.

Steam-style Beer

A full-flavored steam beer with a hearty flavor. Steam beer is lager brewed and aged at room temperature. Drink after 3 weeks aging for the finest flavor.

    6 lbs. light American malt extract
    1 lb. crushed amber crystal (lovibond 40), steeped before the boil
    First flavoring: 1 ¼ oz. Northern Brewer or Perle (8.75 AAU's)
    Second flavoring: ¾ oz. Cascade (3.3 AAU's)
    Aromatic: ½ oz. Cascade (2 AAU's)
    1 teaspoon gypsum
    1 teaspoon Irish moss
    Lager yeast liquid starter or dried lager yeast
    4 ½ oz. corn sugar for carbonation

Starting gravity: 1.044, finished at 1.012 or less.

Light Lager

Light lager is the most difficult to brew at home, as it requires refrigerated aging and high quality lager yeast. For an authentic flavor, fermentation temperature should be steady and no higher than 65 degrees F. After bottling, leave at fermentation temperature for 6 days to allow carbonation to build, before refrigerating for at least 4 weeks.

    6 ½ lbs. light malt extract (as light as possible)
    First Flavoring: ½ oz. Hallertau hops (2 AAU's)
    Second Flavoring: ¾ oz. Hallertau hops (3 AAU's)
    Aromatic: ¼ oz. Saaz (1.25 AAU's)
    1 teaspoon gypsum
    1 teaspoon Irish moss
    Lager yeast liquid starter or dried lager yeast
    4 ½ oz. corn sugar for carbonation

Starting gravity: 1.045, finishes at 1.012 or less.

8 Brewing Instructions

1. Before brewing, determine the 5 gallon level on your fermenter (if it is not already marked) by filling it with 5 gallons of water. Either mark this level with a crayon or measure how many inches it lies below the rim. Sterilize the fermenter with diluted bleach solution (see chapter 2), rinse, and cover loosely.

2. Prepare your yeast. If using liquid yeast, start according to instructions (it takes 2 days or longer to incubate). If using dry yeast, mix the contents of your yeast packet with 1 cup of 95 to 105 degree water to rehydrate (be sure to sterilize the cup beforehand). Cover to prevent contamination by airborne bacteria.

3. To at least 2 gallons of warm water in a 3 gallon or larger boiling pot, add the gypsum water treatment. If you are using crushed flavoring malts, such as black patent or crystal, enclose them in a steeping bag and add to the boiling pot. Turn on the burner and let the flavoring malts steep in the pot like tea as it comes to a boil. Once the pot is on the verge of boiling, remove the flavoring malts and discard. Do not boil the flavoring malts, as boiling can leech harsh tannin flavors from the malt husks.

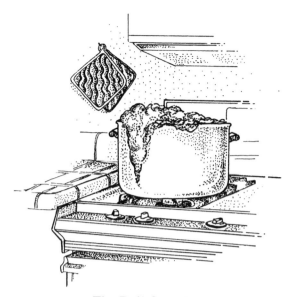

The Boil Over Blues

4. Once the pot comes to a boil, turn off the heat and add the malt extract (and sugar if used), stirring vigorously to keep it from burning on the bottom. Once the malt is dissolved, turn on the heat. In 15 to 20 minutes, the pot will come to a boil. Warning - sugary malt solution boils over readily in concentrated solutions, especially just when coming to a boil, so watch the pot carefully. A gas stove is preferable because the heat can be shut off instantly to avert a frothy eruption. If you use an electric stove, be prepared to slide the brew kettle off the element. Blowing on the rising foam while stirring can help reduce foaming.

5. After the pot comes to a second boil, add the first amount of flavoring hops to add hop bitterness. After 30 minutes, add the second amount of flavoring hops (which primarily provide hop flavor), and 1 teaspoon of Irish moss to promote firm trub settling. Five minutes before the end of the 1 hour boil, add the aromatic hops to provide hop aroma in the finished beer.

6. After the hour boil, turn off the heat and cover the pot tightly with a lid. Ideally the finished wort (unfermented beer) should be cooled as rapidly as possible, to settle out the coagulated protein and hop trub into a firm sediment. To make the unwanted trub settle largely in the middle of the pot (facilitating siphoning from the edge), rapidly stir the hot wort with a sterile spoon; the trub will settle thicker in the center of the pot than on the edges as it cools.

For rapid cooling, place the boiling pot (careful, its hot!) in a sink of cold water. Change the water two or three times in an hour to cool the wort to under 100 degrees F. If you cannot put your pot in a sink, leave tightly covered for 4 to 8 hours to allow for cooling and settling.

7. Once the wort is 95 degrees F. or less, carefully siphon from the edge of the pot into a sterilized fermenter (blow-off style not recommended), being sure to leave as much of the trub sediment behind as you can. Sterilize your siphon hose before use, and fill with clean tap water to start the siphon without mouth contact. If the wort has settled properly (and was stirred to help form a conical sediment prior to cooling) you should only have to leave an inch or so of wort behind. If the trub sediment has not settled fully, it will tend to be kicked up by the siphoning action. In this case, some trub will go up the hose, but try to leave the last inch of sediment behind. After filling the fermenter with wort, add cold water if necessary to reach the 5 gallon mark.

8. Stir in the yeast with a sterilized spoon to begin fermentation and close the fermenter cover. Place the fermenter in a cool place away from direct sunlight, and fill the airlock ½ full.

9. After 12 to 24 hours, fermentation will begin, as indicated by a layer of foam forming on the surface of the wort. In 2 or 3 days, the foam will sink back into the beer. If you plan

to use a secondary fermenter (recommended only for delicate, lightly flavored beers, or when brewing in hot weather), sterilize the secondary at this time and transfer the beer with a sterilized hose into the secondary and seal with an airlock.

10. Nine to eleven days after adding the yeast, the beer will probably be finished fermenting and ready to bottle, unless you are brewing a lager at temperatures under 60 degrees F., which will often take 13 days or more to fully ferment out and settle. Before bottling, it is necessary to take a hydrometer reading to be sure fermentation has finished.

11. Put the sterilized hydrometer into the beer and spin to dislodge any bubbles. The reading is taken at the point where the stem emerges from the beer. If you are brewing an experimental recipe and do not know the approximate finishing gravity, take 2 readings in 3 days to make sure the hydrometer has stopped dropping. If it is still dropping, wait another 3 days and repeat until the hydrometer reading is stable. Warning - if you bottle before the beer has finished fermenting, your bottles could explode.

12. Prepare to bottle. Sterilize your bottles with diluted bleach solution and rinse with water. Add the priming corn sugar (usually 4 to 4½ oz.) to a sterilized priming tank and siphon in the beer, avoiding splashing. Stir the sugar thoroughly into the beer with a sterilized spoon before filling the bottles to leave an inch of headspace below the cap. For ale, age at fermentation temperature for 2 to 3 weeks before drinking; for lager, age at fermentation temperature for 6 days, and then refrigerate until the beer clears (usually in 4 to 6 weeks).

9 Refinements

Gypsum

Gypsum is added to the boil to increase water hardness, facilitating the coagulation of unstable malt protein and the sedimentation of yeast. You can buy water treatment packets containing gypsum or food grade gypsum at home brewing stores.

Irish Moss

Irish Moss (a dried seaweed) is helpful, like gypsum, in removing unstable malt protein from the wort. A protein coagulating agent, the seaweed becomes gelatinous when added to the boil and attaches itself to malt protein before settling out. Add ½ teaspoon of Irish moss during the last 30 minutes of the boil. Irish moss is best used as a complement to gypsum, for firm settling of the boil-coagulated trub.

Fining

Fining is a settling process home brewers use to increase the clarity and reduce the amount of yeast sediment in bottled beer. Ordinary unflavored household gelatine (Knox™, etc.) is made into a solution and stirred into the beer in a secondary fermenter. The gelatine settles out, carrying much of the suspended yeast to the bottom of the fermenter, leaving the overlying beer relatively clear. When bottled, properly fined beer has a sediment layer no thicker than a coat of paint.

To fine your beer, wait until fermentation has largely waned and the beer is very close to finishing gravity. Stir 2 teaspoons of unflavored gelatin into a cup of cool water, let soak for 30 minutes, and then heat to 180 degrees F. before stirring into the beer (ideally, place the beer in a secondary fermenter). Let the gelatin settle for 3 days before bottling in the normal manner.

Records

Keeping an accurate record of each brew is essential if you desire to refine your own recipes and brewing methods. Without written records, you'll awaken to find yourself wondering if the excellent ale you served last night contained 2 or 2¼ ounces of Fuggle hops, and how much crystal grain: was it 8 ounces or 1 pound?

An easy way to prevent confusion is to write the beer's ingredients, yeast addition (pitching) date, starting and finish-

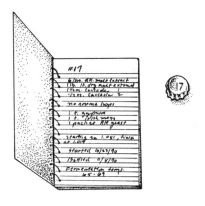

ing gravity, fermentation temperature range, and bottling date in a notebook, assigning a number to each brew. After bottling, write the beer's batch number on the top of the cap with a black felt pen.

This record and labeling system will prevent confusion when trying to duplicate a past success, and bafflement when there are 4 different batches of beer commingling in your crowded refrigerator, each identical in appearance save for the number on the cap.

Beer Glass Preparation

Beer glasses or mugs cleaned with hand dishwashing soap (not dishwashing detergent) are invariably lined with a dry soap film. This residue attacks the beer's frothy head, causing it to collapse shortly after the beer is poured. If you hand wash your glasses, you can scrub them with salt and then rinse with hot water to help eliminate the soapy film. Even more effective is soaking in a dilute mixture of Tri-Sodium Phosphate, a common cleaner available at hardware and paint stores. Make a solution of 3 level tablespoons of TSP in one gallon of warm water and soak your glasses for 1 hour before rinsing with cold water and allowing to air dry. TSP is hazardous: be sure to follow the warning on the box.

Yeast from Commercial Beers

If you live in an area where one of the newer regional brewers sell bottle conditioned beers, you can start the yeast from the sediment in the bottle to pitch your brew. First, get as fresh a sample as you can, buying from a liquor store that probably moves a lot of beer. Be wary of telltale signs of age, such as dust on the shoulder of the bottle. Decant the beer into a glass, stopping just before the thin sediment

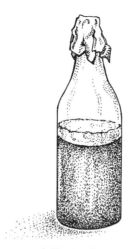

A Yeast Starter

starts to pour out of the bottle. Replace the cap on the bottle loosely and drink the beer. If the beer tastes clean, without yeasty or sour overtones, it is worth making a yeast starter.

A yeast starter is a nutrient broth into which a small amount of inactive yeast is placed to grow into enough active yeast to pitch 5 gallons of wort. The starter must be sterile, as any bacteria in the starter will grow faster than the yeast and ruin your beer. Keep the cap loosely on the beer bottle and divert your bacteria-laden breath from the work area.

To prepare, add 2 tablespoons of dry malt extract (or 2 ½ tablespoons of syrup malt extract) and 3 hop pellets to 2 cups of boiling water. Boil for 20 minutes to sterilize, and then cover and let cool to 85 degrees. When cool, pour the starter mix into the beer bottle and fashion an airlock by crumpling a small amount of aluminum foil over the neck. Place in an area with a temperature of 60 to 80 degrees and wait 1 to 3 days for a head of foam (approximately ¼" thick) to rise in the bottle. When the foam rises, add the starter to 5 gallons of wort within 2 days to start fermentation.

10 Problems

If the instructions are carefully followed (especially the sterilization procedures and temperature guidelines) problems should be few and far between.

Apparent stuck fermentation

Problem: Fermentation appears to proceed vigorously for a few days and then die out.

Solution: Check the beer with a hydrometer. Usually it is fine, and the actual fermentation has almost ceased because the fermentable sugars have largely been eaten by the yeast. If the hydrometer reads near finishing gravity, the beer is probably fine. However, it still needs to sit for a few additional days to give the yeast a chance to settle out of the beer before bottling.

A real stuck fermentation is when the specific gravity is near starting gravity, and does not drop over a period of 3 to 4 days. Stuck fermentations are usually caused by dramatic temperature variations (20 or more degrees in a day) which can shock yeast, rendering it unable to continue. To fix a true stuck ferment, additional fresh yeast must be added, and the beer placed in an area with a very steady temperature. True stuck fermentations are very rare with all malt beers.

Lack of Carbonation

Problem: Fermentation in the bottle has probably been hindered by low (under 55 degrees F.) or unsteady aging temperatures in the first 3 weeks after bottling.

Possible solution: Transfer remaining bottles to an area with steady aging temperature of at least 58 degrees F. and wait two weeks. The yeast will often revive and carbonate the beer.

Too Much Carbonation

Problem: The beer was bottled before fully fermenting out, or has been infected with wild yeast (wild yeast infections are usually accompanied by a yeasty off flavor).

Possible solution: Chill the beer and pour into a pitcher to release excess carbonation before serving.

Sour Or Acidic Flavors

Problem: Bacterial and or wild yeast infection in beer because of unsterile conditions during fermentation. Infection can be introduced by poor quality strains of brewing yeast.

Solution: The only solution is to sterilize more thoroughly when making your next batch (and perhaps switch to a higher quality yeast).

The Ferment Overflows the Airlock

Problem: Caused by a very vigorous ferment in warmer weather. With a plastic fermenter this is more of a mess than a problem, because the beer is generating large volumes of CO_2 gas when overflowing, and CO_2 gas protects the surface of the beer from oxidation and bacterial growth.

WARNING: When using a glass fermenter, an overflowing airlock can be dangerous, as the airlock could clog, possibly causing the bottle to explode.

Possible solution: Cool the beer down by placing it in a water bath to buffer the extremes in temperature.

White Film on the Surface

Problem: Caused by an airborne mold. Appears as a dusty white (very thin) film in the fermenter, and then appears again in the bottled beer. White film mold is not usually accompanied with a taste defect, so it is okay to drink the beer.

Possible solution: Sterilize all your equipment thoroughly before making the next batch. White film mold can be pervasive in parts of the country during the wetter months, so sterilize thoroughly and shield your wort from air contact as much as possible.

Chill Haze

Problem: The beer is clear when at room temperature, but develops a haze when chilled. This is normal for most beers; commercial brewers either filter out the haze or add settling agents, or lager the beer long enough at 48 degrees or less (4 weeks or more) so the haze settles naturally.

Possible solution: Cold aging for 4 weeks or more will settle out the haze. Home brewing stores also sell chill haze adsorbents (silica gel, Polyclar™) that work fairly well in removing the bulk of the haze without the need for refrigeration. Like finings, chill haze adsorbents are usually stirred into the beer in the secondary fermenter a few days before bottling.

Appendix

Average Extract

Average specific gravity produced by adding 1 pound of the ingredient listed below to 1 gallon of water.

Granulated Cane Sugar	1.042
Brown Sugar	1.042
Corn Sugar	1.040
Dry Malt Extract	1.040
Syrup Malt Extract	1.034
Steeped flavoring malts	1.016

Hops

Average alpha acid (potential bittering) content. This can vary by as much as 20% from crop to crop, so it is best to buy hops with the alpha acid level printed on them, or ask your home brewing supplier for the alpha acid content.

Bullion	7.5%
Galena	11.5%
Cascade	4.5%
Chinook	11.0%
Cluster	7.0%
Fuggle	4.5%
Golding	5.0%
Hallertau	4.0%

Mount Hood 4.0%
Northern Brewer 7.0%
Perle 7.0%
Saaz 5.0%
Styrians 6.0%
Tettnanger 4.0%
Willamette........................ 4.0%

Temperature Conversion

To convert a centigrade reading to fahrenheit (approximate), multiply the centigrade temperature by 1.8 and add 32.

To convert a fahrenheit reading to centigrade (approximate), subtract 32 from the fahrenheit reading and divide by 1.8.

Fluid Measure Conversion

To Convert	Multiply By:
Liters to U.S. gallons	0.2642
U.S. Gallons to liters	3.7853
Imperial (British) gallons to U.S. gallons	1.2009
U.S. gallons to imperial gallons	0.8327

Weight Conversion

To Convert	Multiply By:
Grams to ounces	0.0353
Ounces to grams	28.35

Alcohol Conversion

To Convert	Multiply by:
Alcohol by weight to alcohol by volume	1.25
Alcohol by volume to alcohol by weight	0 .8

Gravity Conversion

Home brewers typically use the specific gravity scale when measuring wort density, while commercial brewers commonly use the balling scale.

Balling	Specific Gravity
0	1.000
.5	1.002
1.0	1.004
2.5	1.010
3.0	1.012
4.0	1.016
5.0	1.020
6.0	1.024
7.0	1.028
8.0	1.032
9.0	1.036
10.0	1.040
11.0	1.044
12.0	1.049
13.0	1.053
14.0	1.057
15.0	1.061
16.0	1.065
17.0	1.069
18.0	1.074
19.0	1.078
20.0	1.081

Glossary

ALE A top-fermented English-style beer.

CHILL HAZE A cloudiness that forms in unfiltered beer when it is refrigerated.

DRAFT Beer served from bulk containers.

KRAUSEN (pronounced Kroy-sen) To prime a beer with actively fermenting wort instead of sugar.

LAGER A bottom-fermented beer, aged under refrigeration.

LOVIBOND A system for rating flavoring malts by their darkening effect. If a malt has a higher rating, it will impart a darker color. Crystal (caramel) malts typically have ratings from 20 to 120 Lovibond.

LUPULIN The pollen of the female hop plant, containing a sedative and flavoring oils.

MASHING Reaction between enzymes and starch which produces fermentable sugars from malted barley.

BOTTLE CONDITIONED Beer which has been carbonated by the action of the yeast in the capped bottle as opposed to beer carbonated by the injection of carbon dioxide gas.

PITCHING The addition of yeast to cool wort to start fermentation.

PRIMING The addition of a small quantity of sugar prior to bottling to provide food for the yeast to produce carbonation.

SPARGE To wash by sprinkling with water.

SPECIFIC GRAVITY A hydrometer scale used to measure the amount of fermentable sugars and malt compounds in beer.

WORT (pronounced wert) Unfermented beer.

Bibliography

Berry, C.J.J., Home Brewed Beers and Stouts, 6th edition, The Amateur Winemaker, Hampshire, England 1971.

Burch, Byron Brewing Quality Beers, Joby Books, Fulton, California 1986.

Eckhardt, Fred, The Essentials of Beer Style, Fred Eckhardt Publications, Portland, Oregon 1989.

Fix, George, Hop Flavor in Beer, from Beer & Brewing Volume 8, Brewers Publications, Boulder, Colorado 1988.

Jackson, Michael, The New World Guide to Beer, Running Press, Philadelphia, Pennsylvania 1988.

Line, Dave, Brewing Beers Like Those You Buy, The Amateur Winemaker, Hampshire, England 1978.

Line, Dave, The Big Book of Brewing, The Amateur Winemaker, Hampshire, England 1974.

MBAA (assorted authors), The Practical Brewer, 2nd edition, Master Brewer Association of the Americas, Madison, Wisconsin 1977.

Malting and Brewing Science, Volumes 1 and 2, Second Edition, Chapman and Hall, London, England 1982.

Noonan, Gregory, Brewing Lager Beer, Brewers Publications, Boulder Colorado 1986.

Papazian, Charlie, The Complete Joy of Homebrewing, Avon Books, New York, New York 1984.

Thanks to Bob Loveland for help with Dark Cherry Ale.

Index

Oak chips, 27
Off-flavors:
  bacteria related, 60
  caused by yeast, 28,35
  caused by light, 36
Oxidation (see air)

Pale ale:
  defined, 4,5
  recipe, 46
Perle hop, 26
Pilsner beer, defined, 2
Porter:
  defined, 6
  recipe, 48
Priming:
  container, 11
  flavoring with, 21
Protein removal, 32,55

Records, 56
Rice extract, syrup, 21

Saaz hop, 26
Secondary fermenter, 11
Sierra Nevada Brewing Co.,
6
Silica gel, 61
Siphoning, wort, 53
Soap, on beer glasses, 57
Specific gravity:
  determining, 12,13,14
  estimating, 38
Spices, 27
Starting gravity, 37,38
Steam-style beer:
  defined, 3,34,35

recipe, 50
Sterilization, 7,60
Stout:
  defined, 6
  recipe, 48
Strong ale, 6
Styrian hop, 26
Stuck fermentation, 29,59
Sucrose (see cane sugar)
Sugar:
  corn versus cane, 21
  ratio to malt, 20
Summer beer, recipe, 45

Tannin flavors, 51
Temperature:
  during aging, 33,34,35,36
  during fermentation, 28,35
Tettnanger hop, 26
Thermometers, 12
Tri-sodium phosphate, 15,57

Unfermentables, in malt, 38

Vienna malt, 17,18

Water, 29
Wheat beer:
  defined, 4
  recipe, 46
Willamette hop, 26

Yeast:
  from commercial beers, 57,58
  selecting, 28, 44, 60
Yuengling Brewing Co., 6